D0602537

Complete cocktails

Sebastian Reaburn

HINKLER BOOKS

Author: Sebastian Reaburn
Project Manager: Katie Hewat
Art Direction and Cover Design: Diana Vlad
Internal Design: Graphic Print Group
Photography: Ned Meldrum
Prepress: Graphic Print Group

Decorative motif © iStockphoto.com/Siarnei Kaspiarovich
Chocolates © iStockphoto.com/Zoran Kolundzija
Strawberry © Yuri Arcurs/Dreamstime.com
Strawberries © Hpphoto/Dreamstime.com

HINKLER
BOOKS

Published in 2009 by Hinkler Books Pty Ltd
45–55 Fairchild Street
Heatherton VIC 3202 Australia
www.hinklerbooks.com

© Hinkler Books Pty Ltd 2009

3 5 7 9 10 8 6 4 2
11 13 14 12 10

All rights reserved. No part of this publication may be utilized in any form
or by any means electronic or mechanical, including photocopying, recording,
or by any information storage or retrieval system now known or hereafter invented,
without the prior written permission of the publishers.

This book is intended for use by adults of legal drinking age and over.
Hinkler Books Pty Ltd, its agents and representatives take no responsibility
for misuse of the content within.

ISBN: 978 1 7418 4506 8
Printed and bound in China

contents

about cocktails

Fresh fruit and good booze: this is a winning formula, but it needs a little technical skill to bring together some raspberries and vodka and transform them into a delicious raspberry fizz. This is what this book is about: the bringing together of good booze and fresh fruit with a little knowledge to make great cocktails.

Cocktails are all about delicious flavours and just a little indulgence. Cocktails are about the finer things in life, elegance, sophistication and glamour. They can be complicated constructions of booze or simple mixers, but they are always about flavours and are as close to cooking as you can get without a stove.

To make great cocktails there are some essential rules, and some key equipment. There are also a whole bunch of excellent recipes, and some terrible ones. There are cocktails that are easy to make taste great, and cocktails that are very hard to get right.

What we do in this book is explain the skills needed to produce excellent cocktails at home, give you a rundown on the minimum equipment required, and take you through some recipes that serve to explain, teach and break down cocktails so that when you encounter recipes you have never made before, you will be able

to understand them and ensure that you can produce them correctly and delectably.

The inspiration for this book is the idea of cocktails at home; about making drinks as good, and often better, than those served in bars around the world. There are a few ideas that we play with while covering a bunch of recipes. To begin, we look at each spirit and the drinks that you can make with them, then we match that spirit to some seasonal fruit and produce. Because there is one thing that every good restaurant and every good bar knows: good fresh products are the secret to great food and drink. Within these two structures we will start to explore the idea of flavour matching so that you can quickly match a product or a fruit to a set of flavours and, from there, create delicious drinks.

Cheers

early cocktails

Before we begin talking about cocktails, where they come from and what makes them so delicious, you need a drink in your hand.

One very simple, classical and downright flavoursome cocktail is the Tom Collins. It appeared sometime in the early half of the nineteenth century when fizzy soda water was a new, amazing and health-giving ingredient. A Tom Collins is like a classic home-style lemonade, with a generous helping of gin. It can also be made in the glass that you drink it from; the only equipment you need is a spoon to stir it all together.

Take a reasonably sized tall glass (about 300 ml/12 oz), and add 2 shots (50 ml/2 oz) of gin. If you do not have a measure for the gin, use the cap of the bottle. The inch-long cap you get on Gordon's, for example, will give you about 1 shot (25 ml/1 oz). The shorter cap on Tanqueray will only yield half that. So two of the longer bottle caps, or four of the shorter ones. Add to that 1 shot (25 ml/1 oz) of freshly squeezed lemon juice. Add 2 teaspoons of caster sugar, or ½ shot (12.5 ml/½ oz) of sugar syrup (sugar syrup is just one part water to two parts dissolved sugar). Pop in a few ice cubes and stir vigorously. Leave the spoon in the glass, add about 75 ml (3 oz) of soda water and, as you remove the spoon from the bottom of the glass, gently mix the gin and lemon through the soda. Add a few more ice cubes to fill the glass then garnish with a slice of fresh lemon and, if you want to be traditional, a maraschino cherry.

Now that you have a drink in hand, a little bit about cocktails and where they came from. When we look at where cocktails originated, we can see what purpose they serve and understand how to present, make and enjoy them in the best way possible.

Cocktails are essentially mixed drinks. They originate, in the crudest form, from the alchemical and magical traditions of Europe, Asia, Africa and, in fact, most of the world. From early on people would mix medicinal herbs and flavours with whatever was at hand to create life-giving, healthy potions to encourage wellbeing. We can still see some of these early alchemical traditions in products like Chartreuse, Benedictine, all types of bitters and even some cocktails.

As civilisation and technology progressed, we started to get very good at concentrating flavours and ingredients. The rise of the perfume industry matches the rise of the alcohol distillation industry because they use a lot of the same techniques. When alcohols are distilled, or concentrated, we get spirits. Initially these spirits were thought to bestow eternal life, and the early words for distillates were all corruptions of 'water of life' in some form or another.

One major drawback with early distilled spirits was that the flavours were anything but enjoyable. They would heat your belly and get your eyes watering, but they didn't taste great. There are two reasons for this. One is that the distillers just weren't successful at getting the bitter and harsh impurities out of the fermented fruit, grain or plant. The other reason is that ethanol, the good alcohol, doesn't taste very pleasant. So when people talk about pure vodka, what they are actually talking about is that tiny, tiny element of impurity that makes the ethanol taste good. Some impurities taste good and others taste bad; the job of the distiller is to actively select the good ones and remove the bad ones. This is a very, very difficult job and we have really only started to improve in the last one hundred years.

Before that, most spirits were pretty harsh and needed the addition of something to make them palatable. These are, in essence, the first cocktails, and they always had a health-giving philosophy behind the selection of ingredients.

Products like Benedictine and Chartreuse are leftovers from this age. The recipes that make them famous are secret, purposely medicinal, and designed to taste delicious when added to water. Gin is also from this medicinal tradition, with the forefather of modern gin, Dutch Jenever, starting its life as a liver tonic. Absinthe was originally a stomach tonic devised to encourage digestion and clarity of thought. Indeed, wormwood was in use for thousands of years before absinthe as a health tonic and mind invigorator.

From this tradition of giving health, vitality and generally putting a spring in your step, we see the first true cocktails begin to emerge in America. Most of these early cocktails started their life as a combination of alcohol, sugar, water and health bitter, like Angostura. Another famous early drink is the julep. The name, and the drink, comes from Arabia via Europe. The word juleb, from Arabia, means a health tonic created by soaking herbs or flavoursome leaves, petals and bark in water. The most common form of this was a drink of water and rose petals, most commonly used nowadays in Turkish delight. From there the word came to Europe where its ingredients morphed into a whole series of health-giving tonics, including wormwood.

The tradition of making a tasty beverage by soaking leaves and flowers in water was slowly replaced by soaking leaves or flowers in alcohol: the creation of what we know today as tinctures. The line between drinking for health purposes and using health as a reason to drink was pretty blurry from quite early on. We do know that in Southern America where the mint julep holds court, the drink is older than cocktails and drunk both for its unique flavour and its health-giving attributes. Remember, this was before there was general access to actual medicine.

modern cocktails

From this humble beginning as a medicinal substitute, cocktails eventually found their place during the eighteenth century as the hallmark of gentlemen, business, and all things sophisticated, educated and wealthy. The 1850s marked the highpoint of cocktail consumption and it is the period from 1850 to 1890 that gives birth to the most famous of the classical cocktails: the Manhattan, the old-fashioned, the sazerac, the crusta and the martini. By the end of the 1890s, the temperance movement in America was starting to gain momentum. Although it would be nearly thirty years till the fateful start of prohibition, the rot had already set in and states were going dry left and right. Here began the decline of cocktails in America.

One of the plus sides to the temperance movement and eventual prohibition of alcohol is that the best bartenders moved to Europe and England to ply their trade. It is no surprise that the Savoy Cocktail Book was published in 1930, after ten years of American bartenders' influence on the British drinking culture. It is from England, France and Italy in the '20s and '30s that we get our next wave of famous classical cocktails: the negroni, the sidecar, the white lady, French 75, bellini and the champagne cocktail.

It was around this period that we saw the emergence of modern bartending, standardised measures, standard equipment and techniques. So here is a good time to begin talking about the skills that mark a true cocktail maker as opposed to a barkeep or home dilettante.

The two cocktails that we have described already come from a time before standard bartending skills existed. Bartenders back then were shaking drinks with two glasses, or two metal mugs pressed together, or stirring, or making batches in bowls, and really anything that was on hand. The two cocktails we've already discussed required a spoon, a glass and some ingredients. They were early drinks that had to be able to be made simply and easily, or their popularity would not have spread. If it was impossible to export a drink from one venue to another, then the drink could not gain the following or notoriety that was needed to survive the last two hundred years.

key skills

muddling or crushing

This is about getting juice and flavour from fresh ingredients.

With the mint julep, it is about bruising the mint enough to extract the oils and flavour, but not so much that it becomes bitter.

With a caipirinha, it is about crushing a lime utterly to release all the juice and the oil from the skin.

With a julep I prefer to use the back of a bar spoon or normal spoon. With a caipirinha I like to use a wooden or plastic muddling stick. A muddling stick is about 20 cm (8 in) long and around 2.5 cm (1 in) in diameter. The thing to remember about the diameter of the muddler is that it fits right to the bottom of the glass.

The two styles of muddling, with the spoon and with a muddler, reflect the hardness of the fruit or herb being muddled. Mint is quite delicate, so it only needs a gentle pressure to crush. A lime is quite firm and requires a good bit of arm action to get all the juice out.

stirring

We have shown a drink that is stirred. With the Tom Collins, the stirring is just to integrate and mix the ingredients. It is served on ice, and will stay chilled pretty well. This type of stirring is just the same as stirring a cup of coffee: as long as you get all the ingredients mixed it will be fine.

There is another type of stirring, however, which is applied to martinis, Manhattans and a host of classic cocktails.

This other stirring is about chilling a mixture of ingredients as much as mixing them. It is also about dilution. The right amount of water from the ice with which you are stirring makes or breaks the cocktail.

The perfect example is the Manhattan.

manhattan

INGREDIENTS

American rye whiskey or Woodford Reserve Bourbon, 1½ shots (37.5 ml/1½ oz)

Italian rosso (sweet red) vermouth, ½ shot (12.5 ml/½ oz)

Angostura bitters, dash

Regan's Orange Bitters, dash (optional)

Maraschino cherry syrup, 1 tsp

METHOD

Bartender's Tip

I prefer Carpano Antica Formula – a highly sought-after red vermouth made to an original recipe dating back to the eighteenth century. Its warming flavours are more intense and rounded – stunning.

Select a large mixing glass, a bit taller than a Collins glass and at least as thick as a rocks glass. (These are usually the glass half of a Boston shaker, which we will talk about in more detail later.) Pour in the whiskey, vermouth, bitters and maraschino cherry syrup. Fill the glass to the top with ice and begin stirring. Be mindful to gently move the ice from the top of the mixing glass to the bottom so that all the ice touches the ingredients. As you stir, the ice will get lower in the glass and the liquid will get higher. The best way to judge when the correct temperature and dilution has been achieved is when the level of the ice and the level of the liquid equalise.

Next you need to strain the liquid into a cocktail (martini) glass, leaving the ice in the mixing glass. You can do this easily with a hawthorn strainer or a julep strainer, both of which are designed to stop ice but allow liquid to flow through.

Now you need to garnish the Manhattan. There are two essential items that are added to a Manhattan as a garnish. One is the ubiquitous cherry on a stick; a maraschino cherry that is. These can be found in the cake section of the supermarket named

glace cherries, maraschino cherries or even cocktail cherries. The final element of a fantastic Manhattan is the twist of orange peel. The orange peel sprays a mist of orange oil over the top of the drink, adding a hint of orange flavour and lifting the other flavours. It really makes the drink. The rim of the glass should then be rubbed with the orange side of the peel, and then the peel can be discarded.

Now drink, and think about New York winter nights, a touch of snow in the air and a blazing log fire. This drink contains all the essential warming winter flavours, sweetness, spices, a clean bitter finish, and a touch of sweet orange and maraschino.

cutting a twist

This applies to lemons, oranges, mandarin, grapefruit and limes. In fact, this can be done with any fruit that retains oil in the skin. Pomegranate will give bitter astringency that can still be nice. Passionfruit will give sharp acidity and that sweet passionfruit perfume. Banana will give you clean astringency and the unique aroma of banana, surprisingly.

So, citrus is by far the most common twist, and the easiest to do. All the other examples need a little creativity to make them look good in a glass...

First, use a sharp knife – the sharper the better. A sharp knife is less dangerous than a blunt one because it is more predictable. I like to use a 10 cm (4 in) serrated paring knife. A serrated knife cannot be sharpened like a straight edge, but in the bar we tend to use them for six to eight months and then get a new one. Once you have your sharp knife, place the fruit on a chopping board with its long axis at right angles to the board. You want to cut from the top to the bottom of the fruit rather than around it. There are some exceptions to this, and I will mention them a bit later. Now cut a strip of peel from the top of the fruit to the bottom, with the knife just below the surface of the peel. The aim is to get a strip that is the same width all the way down, about 1 cm (½ in), and cut a layer so that there is little or no white pith left on the reverse side of the peel. It will take a few attempts to get this right.

Once you have your peel, the trick is to twist it correctly. This is done by holding the peel long ways between the forefinger and thumb of both hands, with the peel-side facing the glass and the pith-side facing you. Now quickly squeeze the peel over the glass, shooting the oils onto the surface of the drink. This will also take a few attempts to get right, but can be mastered reasonably fast. The most important thing to remember about twists is getting the oil onto the drink. As long as this happens, finesse, smoothness and speed are secondary. If the drink tastes great, you can forgive a clumsy twister. If the drink is terrible, then no matter how good the twist is, nothing will redeem the creator.

home bar essentials

There are a few pieces of equipment that are essential to making fast and delicious cocktails.

the shaker

The shaker that seems to be the choice of bartenders is the humble Boston shaker. This is a glass mixing container with a stainless steel mixing tin. The glass fits inside the leading edge of the tapered tin, and as the ice and liquid chill the metal, a very tight seal is formed.

With the Boston shaker, there are a few key tips for using it. First, always add the ingredients together in the glass. Ice should always be the last ingredient you add because it starts to melt as soon as you add it.

When you fit the tin to the glass, try to get one side as flush with the glass as possible, while the other side has the largest gap from glass to tin as possible. If the tin is fitted onto the glass dead straight, then it will be a lot harder to open.

When the tin is on the glass, give it a good sharp tap on the top to lock the tin onto the glass. Now upend the shaker so that the glass is facing up. This ensures that the weight of the glass serves to reseal the shaker as you shake.

Hold the shaker with one hand at the top and one hand at the bottom so that it is as secure as possible. When shaking a shaker, there are two things to remember. First, shake it hard. You want to mix the ingredients and agitate the ice. One way of thinking about this is to get as much life as possible into the drink. Secondly, the movement of the shaker must be longer than the shaker. Now that the drink is mixed, enlivened, shaken and generally ready to drink, you have to get it out. This is where most of the problems occur. To open a Boston shaker, hold the metal tin at the bottom with one hand, with the straightest side pointing towards you. Now give the top of the tin a firm slap with the heel of your hand about ninety degrees from the straight side, and above the point where the glass meets the tin. This should loosen it. This is another skill that needs a little practice to get comfortable with.

Once the shaker is open, with the liquid in the metal tin, you apply the hawthorn strainer to the tin. It should fit neatly on the top of the tin so that when you pour out the liquid, all the ice will stay in the shaker. Pour out your drink and garnish.

citrus juicer

The most essential item in any home bar is the citrus juicer. Fresh lemon and lime juice will make a huge difference to the quality of your cocktails. Never succumb to buying juice concentrates or pre-prepared sour mix. All those products contain preservatives, sweeteners and very little of the natural acids that give fresh citrus juice its unique taste.

My favourite citrus juicer is the 'Mexican elbow' or manual lime press. Ask around for a hand lime press, and you will find that they come in three sizes: for limes, lemons and oranges. The best ones seem to be the coloured ones rather than the aluminium ones. To use them, just cut your citrus in half crossways, then place in the press with the cut side facing the extraction holes and the peel facing the press side. As you close the press, the juice will run out the holes as the lime or lemon is effectively turned inside out.

bar spoon

A bar spoon is very nice and professional-looking, but a long spoon of any kind works just as well, as does the back of a fork.

jigger

Jiggers are the little egg-cup-like measuring devices used by bartenders to ensure that they know how much of everything they are putting in. You do not need to buy an actual jigger: any small cup will work just as well, as will the longer lids from a bottle of rum. The important thing about cocktails is that all recipes are ratios, so as long as you use the same measure for all the ingredients, it does not matter if it is a perfect shot, as long as you get the ratio right.

glassware

This is an essential part of making cocktails at home. A good number of martini glasses, a few sling or large, tall glasses, and some good big rocks glasses are the bare minimum. Having said that, they do not have to match, and small wine glasses can double as martini glasses if required. But as a cocktail has to go into something, a good collection of glasses should be a priority.

booze

Don't go out and try and stock a full bar, unless you really want to. The best way to get a good stock of booze is to buy the ingredients for one cocktail, then make that for yourself and friends. If you like it, keep those ingredients on hand. If it is a cocktail that you do not like, see what other drinks can be made from the same basic ingredients. You may need to buy one or two more items, but if they enable you to make a cocktail you love, then it is worth it.

Slowly build up the cocktails you know how to make as you gradually build up your bar. Remember that you do not have to buy full bottles, often half bottles or even miniatures are available to test out a recipe, then, if you like it, go for the big ones.

ice

Ice is the secret and key ingredient of cocktails. You need good quality, clean, fresh, cold ice for making cocktails. This is the reason that cocktails were only for the rich (or those in Alaska) in times past. Ice was a luxury: it was expensive to make, store, ship, move, use and it vanished quickly.

It is fine to make ice in the freezer at home. This is especially good if you are making a cheeky martini or two after work. But there are a couple of tips to making ice. First, tap water is reasonably pure, but tastes better if you run it through a filter. Tap water also has a high proportion of dissolved air in it. This will make cloudy ice that melts quicker and is not as cold. There are two ways to get the air out of water for freezing. The best and most annoying way is to 'double' freeze the ice. Fill your tray, freeze it, get it out, let it thaw completely and freeze it again. The air comes out of solution in the first freezing, it blows away when you thaw it, and the second freezing gives you clear, high-quality ice. The other way is to boil the water, then fill your ice tray and place it in the freezer while still as hot as possible. Both of these will get you very dense, clear, cold ice. But they are not entirely necessary. What is essential, however, is stopping other flavours in the freezer from getting into the ice. I recommend ice trays that are covered or sealed. If you do not have those, then wrap the trays in cling film or place the trays in a plastic bag. This ensures that the frozen fishing bait from that trip you were supposed to go on last year won't flavour your ice. No one enjoys a freezer-smell martini!

When having a party where you will be making loads of drinks, the best option is to buy ice. This ensures that there is enough on hand, and that it is filtered and frozen in an ice machine that has no freezer smell to taint the ice.

For those that want to try something a bit different, try freezing slabs of ice in a plastic tray, or even a lunchbox, and then breaking it up by hand into usable pieces. This type of ice will actually last longer and make drinks colder. The larger pieces take longer to melt and look excellent in a glass.

The best thing you can do when having a cocktail party is ensure a good supply of ice. It eliminates a lot of stress.

cocktail recipes

I have divided the cocktail recipes into seven sections, one for each major spirit, plus a few more. Within that I have split the drinks into those best enjoyed in cooler weather and those best suited to warmer weather. Some cocktails can be enjoyed at any time of year – you'll find these at the beginning of the applicable sections.

All the recipes are set out in a specific style. We give you the name and any quirky or relevant information about the drink. Then we list the ingredients, describe the method of manufacture, what glass it goes into and how, how it should be dressed (the garnish), then where it is good to drink and sometimes with what meal. Sometimes I will provide a tip specific to that drink, or recommend a premium or alternative ingredient that can be used.

I have some preferred spirits that I like to use, but when it says vodka, unless there is a note with a specific reason for a particular vodka, any vodka will do. Just remember: the better the booze and the fresher the ingredients, the better the drink. With liqueurs and other alcoholic ingredients, it is sometimes necessary to go for a specific brand because of bigger flavour differences between some brands, and sometimes it is only available from one producer, like Chartreuse or Benedictine.

❄ Recipes to enjoy with cooler weather

☀ Recipes to enjoy with warmer weather

gin

gin martini

The martini is one of the best-known classical cocktails ever and can be enjoyed at any time of the year. Although it started life around the 1870s, its real heyday was during the 1920s and after the repeal of prohibition. From there it went from strength to strength throughout the 1950s, and in the 1960s its position as the pre-eminent cocktail was set in stone when it became the beverage of choice of the world's most famous spy, James Bond. I like my martinis very dry with a twist of lemon peel and stirred. So that's where we will start.

INGREDIENTS

Tanqueray gin, 2 shots (50 ml / 2 oz)
Noilly Prat vermouth, 1 tsp (¼ oz)

METHOD

Bartender's Tip

A lot of bartenders prefer to coat the ice in the mixing glass with vermouth, pour off the excess vermouth, and then add the gin. I don't do this because the vermouth starts melting the ice on contact, and I find that you have to be a lot quicker and more accurate to pick that perfect moment when the water and gin are at the correct ratio.

In a mixing glass, pour two shots of gin. You can use more if you would like a larger drink, but the martini is best drunk when icy cold, and the larger the drink the faster you have to drink it to ensure that it is cold right through to the end. A double shot martini is about the right size for me to get down before dinner with a little light conversation. Now take your martini glass, fill it with ice and add a splash of dry vermouth. While the glass chills, fill the mixing glass with ice and begin to stir.

As with the Manhattan, the martini is approximately ready when the level of the ice and the level of the gin meet in the middle of the mixing glass. As long as you filled the mixing glass to the absolute top!

Tip the ice and vermouth out of your martini glass, now nicely chilled, and strain in the cold gin.

Garnish with a twist of lemon peel, rubbed on the rim of the glass and dropped into the drink. Remember to get the lemon oils onto the surface of the drink.

For those of you who prefer an olive or two, follow the same method, but abandon the lemon peel and replace it with two good quality green olives on a toothpick: one for the start of the martini and one for the end. Try experimenting with different green olives, including stuffed, whole and pitted. The style of olive will change the nature of the martini quite a lot. Black olives are generally a bit too astringent to work as well as the green, but the choice is yours.

For a dirty martini, there are two methods: the standard and the filthy. For a standard dirty martini add two teaspoons (⅓ oz) of olive brine to the gin while stirring. Then complete the method as normal, and garnish with three olives on a larger toothpick.

For a filthy martini, start with an olive at the bottom of the mixing glass. Add your two teaspoons of brine (⅓ oz), then crush the olive with a muddler. Now add you gin, ice and stir. This will give you a cloudy, muddy looking beast that is best served to those whose fondness for olives exceeds their passion for gin. In both of the above, chill and line the glass with vermouth as normal.

Now sip carefully, but deeply, and enjoy the most sophisticated and world-renowned cocktail of them all.

imperial cocktail

Now the original of this drink, which is another old, old cocktail, calls for equal parts gin and dry vermouth with a dash of maraschino liqueur and a lemon twist. But I have played about with it and still prefer the recipe that was given to me years ago by Wayne Collins, one of the godfathers of the London cocktail renaissance.

INGREDIENTS

Tanqueray gin, 1¾ shots (44 ml/ 1 ¾ oz)

Italian rosso (sweet red) vermouth, ½ shot (12.5 ml/ ½ oz)

Luxardo maraschino brandy, ½ shot (12.5 ml/ ½ oz)

Regans' Orange Bitters, dash (optional)

METHOD

Fill a martini glass with ice to chill it. If you have a large fridge or freezer, you can keep martini glasses there to cut out this step.
In a mixing glass add all the ingredients. Fill with ice. Stir until the level of the ice and the level of the liquid merge.
Tip the ice from your martini glass and strain in the imperial. Garnish with a twist of orange peel.

Drink beside a roaring fire while rain and sleet hammer uselessly at the windows.

princeton

This is one of my favourite winter drinks: one that allows the subtle botanicals in the gin to give you a drink of spices, complexity and a hint of sweetness.

INGREDIENTS

Tanqueray gin, 1½ shots (37.5 ml/1½ oz)

Ruby port, ½ shot (12.5 ml/½ oz)

Angostura bitters, dash

Fee Brothers West Indian Orange Bitters, dash (optional)

METHOD

While you chill a martini glass, pour all the ingredients into a mixing glass.
Fill the mixing glass with ice and begin to stir.
When the ice and the liquid achieve equilibrium, then you are ready to toss out the ice that is cooling the glass and fill your cold, cold martini glass with this delicious mixture.
Garnish with a twist of orange peel.

Drink quickly for a warming aperitif when in old London town.

Bartender's Tip
No other fortified wines work as well with this drink as genuine Portuguese ruby port.

strawberry friday

This is a cocktail that sprang up one spring Friday in Melbourne and, without any effort on the part of myself, swept from bar to bar. As the bartender who created it, there is tremendous pride when your cocktail finds its way onto other menus, at other venues, all by itself.

INGREDIENTS

Strawberries, 6 small or 3 large
South Gin, 1½ shots (37.5 ml/1 ½ oz)
Strawberry liqueur, ½ shot (12.5 ml/½ oz)
Fresh lemon juice, 1 shot (25 ml/1 oz)
Grenadine, ⅓ shot (8 ml/⅓ oz)
Ginger ale, 3 shots (75 ml/3 oz)

METHOD

Cut your strawberries in half and remove the leaves. Place them in a shaker and muddle till they have formed a thick paste. Add all the ingredients except the ginger ale. Top with ice and shake the blazes out of it. Open the shaker and pour the whole lot – ice, strawberries and everything – into a large Collins glass. Top with ginger ale. Garnish with a lemon slice, straws and half a strawberry.

Drink quickly with friends for a perfect after-work restorative.

aviation

This drink is a personal favourite of mine that has been much abused over the decades. It first reared its innocent head around 1916. The drink was created to celebrate the new aviation industry, and in its original form was a delicate pale blue colour. The colour came from Crème de Yvette, a violet liqueur now sadly extinct. After the death of the violets, the drink was made popular in post-prohibition America and quickly spread to London. Without the violet it is a good drink, but with the violet it is sublime. Luckily there are now a few violet liqueurs available with a little searching, although they lack the intense colour of the original Yvette and the aviation has yet to be seen in its pre-war blue splendour.

INGREDIENTS

South Gin or Hendrick's Gin, 1½ shots (37.5 ml/1½ oz)
Luxardo maraschino liqueur, ⅓ shot (8 ml/⅓ oz)
Monin Crème de Violette, ⅓ shot (8 ml/⅓ oz)
Fresh lemon juice, 1 shot (25 ml/1 oz)
Sugar syrup, ¼ shot (6 ml/¼ oz)

METHOD

Pour all ingredients into a cocktail shaker and shake like there's no tomorrow! Strain into a cocktail glass. Garnish with a maraschino cherry.

Drink quickly, but be warned, this cocktail goes down very, very easily!

Bartender's Tip

The heavy juniper of Tanqueray can be a bit much in this drink but, as always, use the gin you have on hand. The Monin Crème de Violette is well worth the search.

french 75

This is an awesome, refreshing drink from the Great War. The name comes from the French 75 mm field gun, a major innovation with heavy artillery. The French, the English and the Americans used it when they entered the Great War a few years later. The drink popped up in England around the mid 1920s, and celebrated the allies' alliance: the gin from England and the champagne from France. Lemons just because they taste fantastic.

The drink was originally served over ice in a very large glass, probably because the people drinking them were military types who like a big drink. Nowadays it is served in a champagne flute and, for myself, amply sufficient as a fresh summer aperitif before dinner.

INGREDIENTS

South Gin, ½ shot (12.5 ml/½ oz)
Fresh lemon juice, ½ shot (12.5 ml/½ oz)
Sugar syrup, ⅓ shot (8 ml/⅓ oz)
Taittinger champagne,
3½ shots (87.5 ml/3½ oz)

METHOD

Pour the gin, lemon and sugar into a champagne flute. Stir to ensure that the sugar is well mixed into the gin and lemon juice. Slowly pour in the champagne till the glass is full.
Garnish with a twist of lemon peel.

Drink in evening wear before a night at the opera.

southside

This is a prohibition drink, and indeed one of the few great cocktails to come from the US at that time. The southside is fresh, crisp, clean and delicious. It was created either in Chicago by bootleggers, or in New York by members of the Southside Sportsman's Club. There is evidence to support both versions of history, but I am convinced that it was created by the country club set in New York rather than a gang of violent beer bootleggers who seemed to have no connection to the sale of illicit gin whatsoever.

INGREDIENTS

South Gin, 1½ shots (37.5 ml/1½ oz)
Fresh lemon juice, ¾ shot (19 ml/¾ oz)
Sugar syrup, ¼ shot (¼ oz)
Mint leaves, 6 large or 8 small

METHOD

Pour all the ingredients into a cocktail shaker, including the mint. Fill the shaker with ice. Shake hard to break up the mint and mix through the ingredients. Strain through both a hawthorn strainer and a fine strainer (a tea strainer) into a chilled martini glass. The tea strainer is to ensure that the small pieces of broken up mint do not wind up in the glass.
Garnish with a sprig of fresh mint.

Drink fast, before the G-men break in the speakeasy doors.

negroni

One of the most-loved aperitif-style classics out there. It is refreshing, but has some healthy bitterness from the Campari that cleanses the palate.

INGREDIENTS

Campari, 1 shot (25 ml/1 oz)
Tanqueray gin, 1 shot (25 ml/1 oz)
Sweet Italian vermouth,
1 shot (25 ml/1 oz)

METHOD

This little drink can be served either straight up or on the rocks. Both begin by pouring all the ingredients into a mixing glass. Fill with ice and stir. When the ice and liquid equalise, either strain into a chilled martini glass, or strain over fresh ice into a rocks glass.
Garnish with a twist of orange peel. On the rocks, add a slice of fresh orange as well as the peel.

Sip slowly, allowing the sweetness of the vermouth to coat your palate, the citrus of the gin to cleanse it, and the bitter Campari to prepare you for another sip.

ramos fizz

This is a New Orleans classic from the last decades of the 1800s. It was the signature drink of the Ramos brothers and made the Hoffman House famous. The exact recipe and method of creation are involved and time consuming, but it is possible to mix it fast and well using a little twenty-first century know-how. Originally the drink contained orange flower water, a baking and cooking ingredient that is actually harder to find than orange bitters.

INGREDIENTS

Tanqueray gin, 2 shots (50 ml/2 oz)
Regan's Orange Bitters, dash
Sugar syrup, ⅓ shot (8 ml/⅓ oz)
Egg white, ¼ shot (6 ml/¼ oz) (optional)
Maraschino liqueur, ¼ shot (6 ml/¼ oz)
Fresh lemon juice, 1 shot (25 ml/1 oz)
Thin cream, 1 shot (25 ml/1 oz)
Soda water, 2 shots (50 ml/2 oz)

METHOD

This seems like a tricky drink, but if you follow the recipe and method, it will work well. The drink should be light and fluffy, with a soft lemon zestiness and a creamy texture. The soda gives a tiny spritz to the finish, like a delicious adults-only lemon and gin spider.
Pour all the ingredients into a cocktail shaker except the soda water. Do not add ice.
Shake really hard for fifteen seconds. Open the shaker, fill it with ice and shake again for fifteen seconds. Strain into a tall glass with no ice. Topped with soda water, it should fizz up even more.
Garnish with a maraschino cherry dropped through the foam. The texture is right when the cherry takes longer to sink to the bottom than it takes to drink the drink, but then I drink quite fast.

Drink quickly as a muggy autumn restorative, or the hangover cure it was originally created as.

vodka

vodka martini

The classic straight booze vodka drink is of course the vodka martini. This version gained popularity right through the 1950s until immortalised by James Bond with both the vespa and the shaken vodkatini.

INGREDIENTS

42 Below Vodka, 2 shots (50 ml/2 oz)
Noilly Prat dry vermouth, dash

METHOD

There are two options with this, shaken or stirred. For those who want to recreate the Bond style, then it has to be shaken, but don't shake too long! You can easily over dilute the drink and serve a watery martini. I prefer it stirred, but then I also prefer a lemon twist, so don't believe everything I have to say...

Pour the vodka into a mixing glass or cocktail shaker. Fill with ice and either begin to stir, or shake.
If you are stirring, then it will be ready when the liquid and the ice merge.
If you are shaking, then about five seconds is generally enough.
As before, prepare your martini glass with a dash of the vermouth and some ice to chill it.
When the martini is ready, tip out the vermouth and ice, and refill with the clear, cold, delightful and strong martini.

Garnish with a twist of lemon peel, rubbed on the rim of the glass and dropped into the drink. Remember to get the lemon oils onto the surface of the drink.

Now put on a tuxedo or dinner suit, check your Astin Martin is where you left it, and sip, savouring the crisp cold vodka.
For those who prefer an olive, feel free. The method for a dirty vodkatini or even a filthy one remains the same. (Refer to gin martini for exact instructions.) When serving a vodka martini with olives I prefer to use a more full-bodied vodka like Grey Goose. The smoothness and delicacy of 42 Below and Ketel One are a little overwhelmed by the olives. If you can find it, there is an Estonian vodka called Tall Blond that suits olives fantastically.

espresso martini

A Dick Bradsel drink, originally called the stimulant, the espresso martini was created in the mid '90s and very quickly gained a huge following. In the days before energy drinks, this was the cocktail that would famously wake you up, then mess you up.

INGREDIENTS

42 Below Vodka, 1½ shots (37.5 ml/1½ oz)
Fresh espresso, 1 shot (25 ml/1 oz)
Kahlua, ½ shot (12.5 ml/½ oz)
Sugar syrup, ¼ shot (6 ml/¼ oz)

METHOD

Pour all ingredients into a cocktail shaker. Fill with ice, and shake, shake, shake like you have never shaken before! Strain into a martini glass. Garnish with three coffee beans in the classic Italian tradition, one each for wealth, health and happiness.

The cocktail should be a foamy rich gold when you pour it, and this should slowly settle upwards until you have a thick head of cream. This is a great drink to practise your shaking with: it very clearly rewards hard, fast shaking and shows when you need to put a little more elbow into it. We use this drink for training new staff about how hard to shake their drinks.

Bartender's Tip

While this drink can be made with other types of coffee, taking into account the dilution from shaking the drink with ice makes espresso the best as it has the highest concentration.
Instead of Kahlua, try Galliano Ristretto for an extra strong drink or vanilla liqueur for something a little more accessible.
You can also try 42 Below Manuka Honey Vodka for something very different.

vespa

This is the original James Bond martini. It should only be mixed by bartenders secretly reporting back to the KGB, and only drunk when wearing a Rolex submariner (or the real James Bond watch described in *Casino Royale* but never named ... the Rolex Explorer 1). Nowadays, of course, an Omega or a Seiko can be substituted.

INGREDIENTS

Smirnoff Black Vodka,
½ shot (12.5 ml/½ oz)
Tanqueray gin, 1½ shots (37.5 ml/1½ oz)
Lillet Blanc, ¼ shot (6 ml/¼ oz)

METHOD

Pour all ingredients into a cocktail shaker, including the vermouth. Fill with ice and shake for about five seconds. Fine strain into a martini glass. Garnish with a twist of lemon peel.

Drink while gambling millions of dollars of other people's money in an attempt to bankrupt a global terrorist organisation. Always remember that too many of these might necessitate defibrillation.

Bartender's Tip

Lillet Blanc is a sweet white vermouth from France. It is a fantastic cocktail ingredient and well worth the search to find it.

chocolate martini

Bartender's Tip

Mozart Black chocolate liqueur from Austria is my favourite for this drink as it retains some of that real chocolate bitterness.

This drink can be a very simple sweetened martini that is well worth drinking, or a sickly sweet creamy monstrosity that should be feared and opposed at every turn.

INGREDIENTS

Ketel One Vodka or Grey Goose Vanilla Vodka,
1½ shots (37.5 ml/1½ oz)
Dark chocolate liqueur, ½ shot (12.5 ml/½ oz)

METHOD

Pour all ingredients into a mixing glass. Fill with ice and stir, or shake if you want (sometimes it pays to put on a bit of a show!). Strain into a martini glass. Garnish with shaved dark chocolate.

For those that want to add just a little something special to this drink, I recommend two variations. First, you can add about ⅙ shot (4 ml/⅙ oz) of dark rum. You will not be able to taste this, but it will lend a depth and richness to the drink without changing the primary flavour.
The other variation is to add a little chilli. Just a ¼ chilli crushed in the shaker and then shaken through will give this a very pleasing zing. Beware of overheating the drink with too much chilli, and fine strain the final drink to ensure that there are no chilli seeds lurking at the bottom of the glass.

moscow mule

This is one of the most classic and simply perfect vodka cocktails out there.

INGREDIENTS

Vodka, 1½ shots (37.5 ml/1½ oz)
Ginger beer, 4 shots (100 ml/4 oz)
2 lime wedges

METHOD

Squeeze the lime wedges into a tall glass. Add ice and vodka, then top with ginger beer. Simple, easy and delicious. Garnish with a sprig of mint if you like.

Bartender's Tip

Smirnoff was the original vodka used for this drink, but feel free to experiment. Ginger ale will not work as a substitute for the ginger beer.

match spring punch

This is a cocktail that has changed a lot since it was first created by Dick Bradsel in the late '90s. Originally called Polish spring punch, it contained no fresh raspberries and crème de cassis instead of crème de framboise. The recipe that I like is the recipe that was made popular by Match Bar, which is fresh, tasty, zingy and decadent.

INGREDIENTS

42 Below Vodka, 1½ shots (37.5 ml/1½ oz)
Crème de framboise (raspberry liqueur), ½ shot (12.5 ml/½ oz)
Raspberries, 8 crushed
Lemon juice, 1 shot (1 oz)
Sugar syrup, ¼ shot (6 ml/¼ oz)
Champagne, 4 shots (100 ml/4 oz)

METHOD

In a cocktail shaker, crush the raspberries, then add everything except the champagne. Fill the shaker with ice and shake hard to ensure that the raspberries mix through. Strain over crushed ice in a large sling glass. Top with champagne. Garnish with raspberries and a lemon wedge.

caiprioska

This drink has become a modern vodka classic. Based on the Brazilian caipirinha, it is simply lime, sugar and lots of vodka.

INGREDIENTS

Lime, 1
Vodka, 2 shots (50 ml/2 oz)
Sugar syrup, ½ shot (12.5 ml/½ oz)
White sugar, 1 tsp

METHOD

Take the lime and cut it into twelve chunks. In a rocks glass, add the white sugar and lime, then muddle until all the juice is out of the lime and the sugar has ground some of the oil from the peel. Then add the vodka, sugar syrup and top the glass with crushed ice. Now churn the mixture to mix the sugar, lime and vodka. Top with a little more crushed ice if required and add a straw.

Drink overlooking the beach.

cosmopolitan

This is perhaps the most ubiquitous cocktail around. It can be found from Melbourne to Las Vegas, from London to Madrid. Perhaps because of this it is made in numerous different ways, some of which are not fit to grace the palate of the least discerning drinker. The Cosmopolitan has a bit of a sordid history, from Miami to New York and from there to the world. The most important recipe is that devised by Toby Cecchini in New York. It is this recipe, or a very similar version, that Dale De Groff made famous and that is very tasty indeed.

INGREDIENTS

Citrus vodka, 1½ shots (27.5 ml/1½ oz)
Cointreau, ½ shot (12.5 ml/½ oz)
Cranberry juice, ½ shot (12.5 ml/½ oz)
Fresh lime juice, ½ shot (12.5 ml/½ oz)
Sugar syrup, dash

METHOD

Add all ingredients to a cocktail shaker. Shake hard, like I know you like to, and strain into a chilled martini glass. Garnish with a twist of orange peel. For those who want to look like a professional, the orange peel should be 'flamed', where the oils are squeezed from the peel over a naked flame, causing a miniature flamethrower.

Drink while gossiping.

Bartender's Tip

The original vodka used for this drink was Absolut Citron, but I like Ketel One Lemon. No other triple sec will work as well Cointreau. To make a slightly more forgiving drink, increase the cranberry juice to a full measure.

lemon three ways

This is one of my own recipes, although it is not a new idea. I am a fan of vodka, and love the crisp citrus hit you get from the first sip, right down to the slightly bitter creamy finish. For me, vodka is perhaps most perfectly matched with fresh lemon!

INGREDIENTS

42 Below Vodka or Ketel One Lemon Vodka, 1½ shots (37.5 ml/1½ oz)
Limoncello, ½ shot (12.5 ml/½ oz)
Lemon juice, 1 shot (25 ml/1 oz)
Sugar syrup, ½ shot (12.5 ml/½ oz)

METHOD

Add all ingredients to a cocktail shaker, and fill with ice. Shake hard. Strain into a chilled cocktail glass.
Garnish with a twist of lemon peel.

Sip slowly, allowing the vodka and the lemon juice to quietly meld together and float across your tongue.

cherry collins

This is an autumn favourite of mine. Cherries are just so delicious.

INGREDIENTS

Vodka, 1½ shots (37.5 ml/1½ oz)
Cherry brandy, ½ shot (12.5 ml/½ oz)
Fresh lemon juice, ¾ shot (19 ml/¾ oz)
Black cherries, 8 pitted
Ginger ale, 3 shots (75 ml/3 oz)

METHOD

In a shaker, muddle the pitted cherries. Add all the other ingredients except the ginger ale. Fill with ice and shake hard enough to mix the cherries and the liquid thoroughly. Pour the whole thing, ice cherries and all, into a large sling glass. Top with ginger ale.
Garnish with a black cherry and a lemon slice.

Drink as one last fruit-filled memory of the summer that has gone.

Bartender's Tip

Use Wisniovska, the traditional Polish cherry vodka, if you want.

tequila

❄ white chocolate toddy

Although it sounds strange, white chocolate and tequila is a match made in heaven. To make this winter warmer you will have to track down some white chocolate syrup (I prefer Monin).

INGREDIENTS

Herradura Blanco Tequila, 1½ shots (37.5 ml/1½ oz)

Monin White Chocolate Syrup, ½ shot (12.5 ml/½ oz)

Hot water, ½ shot (12.5 ml/½ oz)

Regan's Orange Bitters, dash

METHOD

In a mug or heatproof glass, place all the ingredients. Now heat with either a microwave, the steam wand of a coffee machine, or by placing the mug in a saucepan of boiling water. The drink should be good and hot to ward off the snow.

When piping hot, stir gently, and grate a little nutmeg or white chocolate over the top.

For those who want something a little extra special, you can melt some white chocolate into the drink, stirring all the time, but the beverage will then be cloudy.

Bartender's Tip

Others tequilas will work, but Herradura has the most chocolate in it already.

el diablo

This is a tall refreshing tequila drink that still has a little weight and power.

INGREDIENTS

Herradura Reposado Tequila, 1½ shots (37.5 ml/1½ oz)
Fresh lime juice, 1 shot (25 ml/1 oz)
Crème de cassis, ½ shot (12.5 ml/½ oz)
Ginger beer, 4 shots (100 ml/4 oz)

METHOD

In a tall glass add all except the cassis. Fill with ice, stir gently, then float the cassis on the top. It will slowly sink through the drink making a nice pink colour.
Garnish with lime wedges or a mint sprig, or both!

Drink quickly for a recharge.

Bartender's Tip

Ginger ale does work in place of ginger beer, but only just.

fuego verde (green fire)

This cocktail was given to me by Merlin Jerebine, a fervent tequila fan and bartender. It is a perfect spring drink for those days when the sun is shining, but the wind still has a chill to it. This is a refreshing beastie with a healthy hit of spices to warm up your afternoon.

INGREDIENTS

Herradura or Casa Dores Reposado, 2 shots (50 ml/2 oz)
Fresh lime juice, 1 shot (25 ml/1 oz)
Agave syrup, ⅓ shot, (8 ml/⅓ oz)
Green chilli, 1.25 cm (½ in)
Pineapple, 3 cubes about 2.5 cm (1 in)
Mint leaves, 4

METHOD

Add mint, pineapple and chilli to a cocktail shaker. Muddle to extract all the juice. Add all the other ingredients and ice. Shake real hard until you are completely warmed up. Fine strain (using a tea strainer) into a martini glass. Garnish with a split chilli so you can spice it up some more if required.

Drink in the afternoon sun, ignoring the still cold breeze.

Bartender's Tip

Sugar syrup will work if you can't find agave syrup, but not quite as well.

margarita

This is the most well known, most consumed, and most enjoyed tequila drink of them all. It is all about summer, and crisp, fresh and delightful.

INGREDIENTS

Herradura Blanco, 1½ shots (37.5 ml/1½ oz)
Cointreau, ½ shot (12.5 ml/½ oz)
Fresh lime juice, 1 shot (25 ml/1 oz)
Sugar syrup, ¼ shot (6 ml/¼ oz)

METHOD

In a cocktail shaker, add all the ingredients. Fill it with ice and shake to a salsa beat. Strain into a chilled martini glass. Garnish with a salt rim or a lime wedge.
To salt the rim of a martini glass, fill a saucer with good quality salt flakes, not table salt. Now take your chilled glass and rub the outside edge of the rim with a piece of lime. Finally, slowly rotate the glass through the salt with the edge submerged in the flakes. Shake off any excess and you are ready to rock.

Bartender's Tip

Experiment with as many tequilas as you can; they all work well in this one.
You can also experiment with other orange liqueurs to see which one matches your tequila best. Always use fresh juice, never lime cordial! If you are lucky enough to find some, try using agave syrup instead of sugar. You might need a little more, but the flavour is fantastic, especially with the more full-bodied tequilas.

blended margaritas

I rarely recommend a blender, but a blended margarita is a thing of beauty and is extra refreshing. There are a couple of tricks to getting it just right. Using the same recipes as above, increase the sugar a little bit. The blended ice will tend to tone down the flavours, so the extra sugar is needed to bring them back up a bit. Now, the trick to getting a good consistency is to remember that it is easier to add more ice than to take ice away. Usually it requires one-and-a-half times the amount of liquid to achieve that perfect pourable slush that is the hallmark of a perfectly blended margarita. There are some exceptions, however. If you are making two or more at the same time, the extra liquid will cause the ice to melt faster, thus adding more water. When making multiple margaritas, start with less ice and add more as needed to thicken to perfection.

Now, for blended fruit margaritas (my favourite is mango), the recipe needs to change a little.

INGREDIENTS

Tequila, 1½ shots (37.5 ml/1½ oz)

Fruit liqueur (mango, strawberry or whatever you like), ½ shot (12.5 ml/½ oz)

Fresh lime juice, 1 shot (25 ml/1 oz)

Fruit puree (same fruit as your liqueur), 1½ shots (37.5 ml/1½ oz)

Sugar syrup, ½ shot (12.5 ml/½ oz)

METHOD

Place all your ingredients in the blender. Add ice (one-and-a-half times the amount of liquid). Blend until thick and delicious. Pour into a massive martini glass, or even a rocks glass.
Garnish with the appropriate fruit, or just a wedge of lime.

Drink by the pool.

walnut old fashioned

To make this one you will need to track down some walnut liqueur. This is often called Nocino or Nocello if from Italy, or crème de noix or eau de noix if it is from France.

INGREDIENTS

Herradura Anejo, 1½ shots (37.5 ml/1½ oz)

Walnut liqueur, ½ shot (12.5 ml/½ oz)

Angostura bitters, dash

Sugar syrup, ¼ shot (6 ml/¼ oz)

METHOD

In a rocks glass, add the sugar and bitters. Now add ice one cube at a time while stirring gently. Once the glass is at least one-third full of ice, add ½ shot (12.5 ml/½ oz) of the tequila. Keep adding ice and stirring as you add the rest of the tequila. Once the glass is full of ice, pour the walnut over the top and give it a final gentle stir.
Garnish with a twist of orange peel.

Sip slowly; the flavour will improve over time as the ice melts.

rum

rum and raisin

This full-bodied beauty is made using the same method as the walnut old-fashioned, except you need to track down some Pedro Ximenez sherry. Also called PX sherry, it tastes almost exactly like liquid raisins.

INGREDIENTS

Dark rum, 1½ shots (37.5 ml/1½ oz)
PX sherry, ½ shot (12.5 ml/½ oz)
Angostura bitters, dash

METHOD

In a rocks glass, add the PX sherry and bitters. Now add ice one cube at a time while stirring gently. Once the glass is at least one-third full of ice, add ½ shot (12.5 ml/½ oz) of the rum. Keep adding ice and stirring as you add the rest of the rum until the glass is full of ice and rum. Garnish with a twist of orange peel.

As before, sip slowly; the flavour will improve over time.

Bartender's Tip

My favourite dark rum is Inner Circle, which is made in Australia.
No sugar syrup should be needed, but add a little if you have a sweet tooth.

rum shrub

This is a recipe of mine inspired by an early nineteenth-century method of preserving fruit. Traditionally a shrub is like an alcoholic jam that is added to chilled water and drunk for refreshment. These were drinks that existed at the farm rather than the bar, but they make for delicious drinking in any environment.

INGREDIENTS

Appleton Estate VX Rum, 1½ shot (37.5 ml/1½ oz)
Crème de framboise, ½ shot (12.5 ml/½ oz)
Raspberries, 8
Angostura bitters, dash
Sugar syrup, ¼ shot (6 ml/¼ oz)

METHOD

In a cocktail shaker, crush the raspberries, then add the other ingredients. Fill the shaker with ice and shake it hard to break up the raspberries and mix the ingredients. Strain into a martini glass or champagne saucer.
No garnish required.

Drink while surveying your property, even if that consists of just the kitchen and lounge room.

chocolate blazer

This is one for the brave. The method of production used to make a blazer is very entertaining, and quite dangerous. It was perfected near the San Francisco goldfields around 1850. The famous Jerry 'The Professor' Thomas brought the drink to New York where it achieved still more fame and a little infamy. The blazing part of the drink is to pour the liquid from one metal mug to another while it is on fire. This takes a lot of concentration, steady hands and should be practised cold before you risk burning down the house. I also recommend making this drink outdoors, but not anywhere near long grass or petrol stations.

INGREDIENTS

Dark rum (overproof 57%), 1½ shots (37.5 ml/1½ oz)
Mozart Black chocolate liqueur, ½ shot (12.5 ml/½ oz)
Fee Brothers Aromatic Cocktail Bitters (or Angostura), dash
Dark chocolate, 3 squares
Hot water, ½ shot (12.5 ml/½ oz)

METHOD

Now the trick with this drink is to get the liquid heated a bit before trying to light it. This will avoid embarrassing lack of ignition. This particular method and recipe was perfected by Melbourne bartender Stacy Field, who taught me. Take two metal mugs or jugs, as long as they have handles. Pewter mugs are not recommended because they can melt when making this drink. I found that out the hard way...

Fill both mugs one-third with boiling water. In one mug, place a small glass that will sit in the hot water. Into this glass add all your ingredients, allow them to warm and then give it a stir to mix through the chocolate.

Once the liquid is warmed, about thirty seconds is usually enough, take out the glass. Remove the hot water from the two metal mugs. You now have two hot mugs and a small glass of hot cocktail. Now pour the cocktail into one of the hot jugs. Carefully light the liquid. While it is burning, pour it from one jug to the other, being careful not to spill any or burn yourself. Six to eight pours are about what you need, but be careful, because the alcohol will burn first with a small blue flame. As the liquid gets hotter, the sugar and chocolate will begin to join the party, making a much larger yellow flame that can be quite unnerving. When sufficiently 'blazed', pour into a heatproof glass.
Garnish with a dusting of nutmeg and a twist of lemon peel.

Sip very carefully – it will be very hot and will have a lot of alcohol vapours for the first minute or two.

mojito

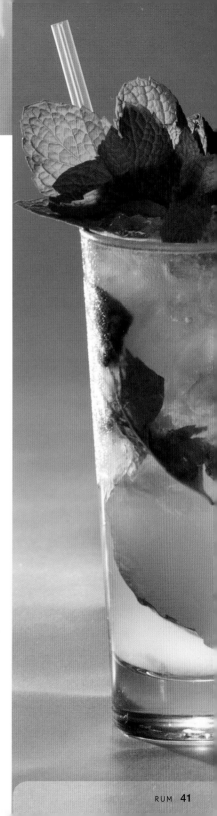

This is one of the most refreshing summer cocktails around. It was made famous in Cuba around the 1920s, but has a far older pirate heritage dating back to Sir Francis Drake. The word mojito loosely translates as 'little soul', meaning the little soul of Cuba, and should therefore contain a Cuban or Cuban-style rum. The most famous Cuban-style rum is, of course, Bacardi. This type of white rum was actually invented and perfected by Facundo Bacardi back in 1862.

INGREDIENTS

Bacardi Carta Blanca, 2 shots
(50 ml/2 oz)

Fresh lime juice, 1 shot
(25 ml/1 oz)

Sugar syrup, ¼ shot (6 ml/¼ oz)

Mint leaves, 6-8

Soda water, 1 shot (25 ml/1 oz)

METHOD

In a tall glass, add the mint leaves and gently crush them. The goal is to gently break the leaves rather than reducing them to a paste. Add all the other ingredients except the soda. Fill the glass three-quarters with crushed ice and churn to mix all the ingredients. Top with the soda water.
Finish with a bit more crushed ice. Garnish with a mint sprig.

Drink while watching the late summer sunset and imagine yourself in Cuba.

daiquiri

This is one of the most famous rum cocktails, and in its most classical form presents one of the best ways to taste and enjoy different rums. Although there is a lot of evidence that the name comes from the daiquiri mines and a beverage served there to refresh the workers, the mixture of rum, sugar and citrus is an old navy and pirate drink. Rum to make the captain's orders palatable, lime or lemon juice to ward off scurvy and sugar to help the medicine go down.

INGREDIENTS

Bacardi Carta Blanca, 2 shots (50 ml/2 oz)
Fresh lime juice, I shot (25 ml/I oz)
Sugar syrup, ¼ shot (6 ml/¼ oz)

METHOD

In a cocktail shaker, add all the ingredients, fill with ice and shake like a pirate. Strain into a martini glass.
Garnish with a lime wedge (optional).

Drink in the shade of a palm after burying your treasure.

Bartender's Tip

Try lots of different rums to taste the differences.

blended daiquiri

This drink has become something of a nightclub special, generally ruined with poor-quality rum, too much sugar and artificial fruit flavourings. To make a really excellent blended daiquiri you can follow the same recipe as the classic, but with a little more sugar. If you want to make a fruit daiquiri, follow the recipe below for a strawberry daiquiri and then you can exchange your favourite fruit for the strawberries if required.

INGREDIENTS

Bacardi Carta Blanca, I ½ shots (37.5 ml/I ½ oz)
Strawberry liqueur (or appropriate fruit liqueur), ½ shot (12.5 ml/½ oz)
Fresh lime juice, I shot (25 ml/I oz)
Sugar syrup, ⅓ shot (8 ml/⅓ oz)
Strawberries, 6 small

METHOD

Add everything to a blender, then add about the same amount of ice as liquid, remembering that it is easier to add more ice than it is to remove it. Blend until a thick liquid is formed that can still be poured. Pour into an oversize cocktail glass, or fancy tall glass. Garnish with cut strawberries.

Drink by the pool.

ice cream treacle

This is a cocktail given to me by Stacy Field, and if you enjoy rum and like vanilla ice cream, then you will love it.

INGREDIENTS

Bacardi 8-year-old rum, 1½ shots (37.5 ml/1½ oz)
Grey Goose Vanilla Vodka, ½ shot (12.5 ml/½ oz)
Monin White Chocolate Syrup, ¼ shot (6 ml/¼ oz)
Fee Brothers Barrel Aged Bitters (or Angostura), dash

METHOD

In a large rocks glass, add the white chocolate syrup and bitters. Now add ice one cube at a time while stirring gently. Once the glass is at least one-third full of ice, add ½ shot (12.5 ml/½ oz) of Bacardi. Keep adding ice and stirring as you add the rest of the rum. Once the glass is full of ice, pour the Grey Goose Vanilla over the top, and give it a final gentle stir.
Garnish with a dusting of nutmeg.

Sip slowly and let the warm flavours melt in your mouth while the rum gently warms your belly.

Bartender's Tip
Other rums can work, but aged white rums like Bacardi 8 are the best.

cognac

brandy alexander

This is one of the most famous cream cocktails around, but it is based on the older gin drink, the Princess Alexandra. I definitely prefer the cognac version.

INGREDIENTS

Cognac, 1½ shots (37.5 ml/1½ oz)

Dark cacao or Mozart Black chocolate liqueur, ½ shot (12.5 ml/½ oz)

Half and half (half cream, half milk), 1 shot (25 ml/1 oz)

METHOD

Add all ingredients to a cocktail shaker, fill with ice and shake it like there is nothing to lose. It is essential with any cream drink that you shake really hard to ensure that the cream is mixed through properly. Strain into a martini glass.
Garnish with a dusting of nutmeg or cinnamon.

Drink after dinner with some expensive chocolates.

❄ between the sheets

This is sort of a variation of the sidecar that I enjoy a lot. It is a little drier, and has less of a citrus bite.

INGREDIENTS

Cognac, 1 shot (25 ml/1 oz)
Bacardi Carta Blanca, 1 shot (25 ml/1 oz)
Cointreau, 1 shot (25 ml/1 oz)
Lemon juice, 1 shot (25 ml/1 oz)
Sugar syrup (optional), ¼ shot (6 ml/¼ oz)

METHOD

Add everything to a cocktail shaker, fill with ice and shake it up. Strain into a martini glass.
Garnish with a twist of lemon peel for extra dry, or a twist or orange peel for a hint of sweetness.

❄

sidecar

This is a European drink from some time during the Great War. The purpose was to create an aperitif, or pre-dinner refresher, that would also ward off a cold. In a lot of ways it works. There is a fresh hit from the orange and lemon, with hidden warmth from the cognac.

INGREDIENTS

Cognac, 1½ shots (37.5 ml/1½ oz)
Cointreau, ½ shot (12.5 ml/½ oz)
Fresh lemon juice, 1 shot (25 ml/1 oz)
Sugar syrup, ¼ shot (6 ml/¼ oz)

METHOD

Add all ingredients to a cocktail shaker. Fill with ice and shake, hard. Strain into a martini glass.
Garnish with a twist of orange peel.

Drink before dinner, when it is warm enough to need refreshment, but cool enough to enjoy the warmth of the cognac.

Bartender's Tip

Despite what others may tell you, the sidecar never had a sugar rim, but it can be quite tasty with one if you really want to.

crusta

Although often listed as the forefather of drinks like the sidecar, the crusta is really a very different beast. It is the first cocktail that had a sugar rim, from where the drink gets it name. The drink popped up around 1850 and was described as better than a cocktail – remembering that, in those days, a cocktail was just water, bitters and spirit. The crusta uses lemon juice not as an ingredient on its own, but as a way of changing the character of the other ingredients.

INGREDIENTS

Cognac, 2 shots (50 ml/2 oz)
Lemon juice, ⅓ shot (8 ml/⅓ oz)
Angostura bitters, dash
Luxardo maraschino brandy, dash
Sugar syrup (optional), ¼ shot (6 ml/¼ oz)

METHOD

Shake all ingredients with ice. Strain into a wine glass filled with crushed ice with a sugar rim or crust. Garnish with an extra long twist of orange peel spiralled into the ice from top to bottom.

Drink quickly, especially in New Orleans where the drink was first created.

champagne cocktail

This is one of the simplest and best drinks around.

INGREDIENTS

Cognac, ½ shot (12.5 ml/½ oz)
Sugar cube, 1
Champagne, 4 shots (100 ml/4 oz)
Angostura bitters, dash

METHOD

Place the sugar cube in a champagne flute. Drop in the bitters and cognac. Fill the flute slowly with champagne.

Drink on special occasions, or to make an occasion special.

camomile punch

This is one of my party drinks, when there are a few people over for cocktails and you still want to be able to sit and talk with them. I usually make this drink in a large teapot or vintage cocktail shaker, but any decent sized jug will do. This recipe serves 4–5.

INGREDIENTS

Strong camomile tea, 10 shots (250 ml/10 oz)
Cognac, 8 shots (200 ml/8 oz)
Cointreau (optional), 2 shots (50 ml/2 oz)
Lemon juice, 4 shots (100 ml/4 oz)
Sugar syrup, 3 shots (75 ml/2 oz) or 6 teaspoons of sugar into the camomile tea

METHOD

Add all ingredients to the teapot, and either add a little ice, or preferably place in the fridge till well chilled. Because the tea is adding a lot of water to the mix, too much ice will dilute the cocktail and make it taste weak and insipid. Pour the punch into tea cups or small glasses.

Sip while playing bridge on the veranda.

rye & bourbon

old fashioned ❄ mint julep

This drink is all about the how, rather than the what. The old fashioned is a cocktail that tests the skill of the bartender: it is about patience rather than show, and sophistication rather than glamour. It is a favourite with most bartenders, and the recipe will work for almost any dark spirit and even some white ones.

Originally you would use a little water and raw sugar, and then spend at least three minutes of your time stirring it until the sugar melted and formed a syrup; but I prefer to pre-prepare sugar syrup.

INGREDIENTS

Woodford Reserve Bourbon, 2 shots (50 ml/2 oz)

Angostura bitters, dash

Sugar syrup, ¼ shot (6 ml/¼ oz)

METHOD

In a large rocks glass, add the sugar and bitters. Now add ice one cube at a time while stirring gently. Once the glass is at least one-third full of ice, add ½ shot (12.5 ml/½ oz) of Woodford Reserve. Keep adding ice and stirring as you add the rest of the bourbon. When the glass is full of ice and bourbon, have a quick taste to ensure that the sugar and bourbon mix is right.

Garnish with a twist of lemon peel if you want to be strictly original, or a twist of orange peel to better match the flavours of the bourbon.

Sometimes you can add a maraschino cherry and a slice of orange as a garnish, but never succumb to the lure of muddling them into the drink. This is a strange modern aberration that doesn't do anything for the flavour.

Yet another classic American whiskey cocktail, the mint julep appears in the South and pre-dates cocktails and cocktail bars. It was created as both a health tonic and as a way of imbibing alcohol that appeared healthy. From these beginnings, probably with brandy or rum, the true mint julep slowly emerged. I have included this because it is a unique flavour, and the personal favourite of a good friend of mine Dane Bottfield. This is his method of creating this fabulous Kentucky staple.

INGREDIENTS

Rittenhouse Rye whiskey, Makers Mark Bourbon or Woodford Reserve Bourbon, 2 shots (50 ml/2 oz)

Mint leaves, 8

White sugar, 1 tsp, or sugar syrup, ¼ shot (6 ml/¼ oz)

METHOD

If you are using sugar, then place it into a large rocks glass or silver julep cup. Add a touch of whiskey and stir, stir, stir until it is dissolved.

Now add the mint and gently crush. Some people advocate crushing the mint into a paste, but this is not needed to release the flavours and can sometimes make the mint slightly bitter.

Fill the glass three-quarters with crushed ice, and pour in the Woodford Reserve.

Now stir the mixture to melt the sugar into the whiskey, and allow the mint to infuse right through the whole drink.

Top with more crushed ice.

Garnish with a massive sprig of mint so that your nose is buried in it when you take a sip.

This drink is drunk with a straw, and inspired the first commercially produced straws in America.

❄

sazerac

This is a quintessential New Orleans cocktail. Created around 1850 and made famous at the Sazerac Coffee House where it was prepared with Sazerac Per Et Fils Cognac. Very quickly people began to use the local rye and bourbon whiskeys. The other essential ingredient in this classic beverage is absinthe. Now that absinthe is finally available again in the Unites States, drinkers there can experience a cocktail that has been pleasing drinkers across the rest of the globe for years.

The recipe that I use is adapted from Dale De Groff's New York sazerac, which uses both cognac and bourbon.

INGREDIENTS

Cognac, 1 shot (25 ml/1 oz)

Woodford Reserve Bourbon or Rittenhouse Rye, 1 shot (25 ml/1 oz)

Le Mercier Absinthe or even Mansinthe, ¼ shot (12.5 ml/¼ oz)

Peychaud's Bitters, dash

Sugar syrup, ¼ shot (6 ml/¼ oz)

METHOD

Take a large rocks glass and fill it with ice. Pour in the absinthe and top it up with water.

This will now chill and season the rocks glass, so that when the time comes to use it, it will have a coating of absinthe to flavour the final drink.

In a mixing glass, add all the other ingredients, fill with ice and stir. As always, the mixture will be about ready when the ice and liquid equalise in the middle of the mixing glass.

Now discard the absinthe and water in the rocks glass. Strain the mixing glass into the seasoned rocks glass. Garnish with a twist of lemon peel, dropped in.

Sip at a reasonable pace while listening to some hot, loose jazz.

Bartender's Tip

Peychaud's Bitters is an American bitters and the only one that works for the sazerac. Please try this drink with just rye or just bourbon. And a quick hint for the New York style, a tiny touch more bourbon than cognac will make for a more balanced drink. The cognac is actually a bit too smooth, and needs a little extra bourbon or rye to combat the powerful flavour of the absinthe.

red berry smash

Another recipe based on the brilliant marriage of bourbon and red berries.

INGREDIENTS

Woodford Reserve Bourbon, 1½ shots (27.5 ml/1½ oz)

Crème de framboise or raspberry liqueur, ½ shot (12.5 ml/½ oz)

Fresh lemon juice, 1 shot (25 ml/1 oz)

Cranberry juice, 1 shot

Raspberries, 6

Sugar syrup, ⅓ shot (8 ml/⅓ oz)

Lemonade, 2 shots (50 ml/2 oz)

METHOD

In a cocktail shaker, crush the raspberries and add all the ingredients except the lemonade.
Fill the shaker with ice, and shake it hard. Pour the whole lot, ice and all, into a tall sling glass. Top with the lemonade. Garnish with a lemon slice and raspberries.

Drink fast for refreshment, or sip slowly to savour the rich flavours.

ginger fizz

This is one of my favourite flavour matches for bourbon or rye whiskey.

INGREDIENTS

Woodford Reserve Bourbon or Rittenhouse Rye, 2 shots (50 ml/2 oz)

Fresh lime juice, 1 shot (25 ml/1 oz)

Ginger, 2.5 cm (1 in)

Sugar syrup, ⅓ shot (8 ml/⅓ oz)

Ginger beer or ginger ale, 3 shots (75 ml/3 oz)

METHOD

In a cocktail shaker, pound the ginger to release the juices. Add all other ingredients except the ginger beer. Fill with ice and shake it really hard to help crush up the ginger. Fine strain into a tall sling glass to remove any pieces of ginger. Top with ginger beer or ginger ale.
Garnish with a slice of ginger and a slice of lime.

Drink carefully, letting the rich whiskey and the hot ginger mingle and mix on your palate.

scotch & irish

rob roy

This is an old twist on the Manhattan.

INGREDIENTS

Dewar's 12-year-old Scotch,
1½ shots (37.5 ml/1½ oz)

Carpano Antica Formula red vermouth,
½ shot (12.5 ml/½ oz)

Angostura bitters, dash

Fee Brothers Orange Bitters (optional),
dash

METHOD

Add all ingredients to a mixing glass. Fill with ice and stir until the ice and liquid meet in the middle. Strain into a chilled martini glass.
Garnish with a twist of orange peel, discarded, and a maraschino cherry on a stick.

Drink in the highlands to ward off the English revenue collectors.

❄ hot toddy

This is the perfect cold cure. As to the true medicinal effects, I am not qualified to report, but it tastes good, makes you feel wonderful and should be taken in moderation.

INGREDIENTS

Jameson 12-year-old Special Reserve,
2 shots (50 ml/2 oz)

Boiling water, 2 shots (50 ml/2 oz)

Fresh lemon juice, 1 shot (25 ml/1 oz)

Honey, ½ shot (12.5 ml/½ oz)

Angostura bitters, dash

METHOD

In a large mug, mix all the ingredients with the boiling water. Sometimes you may need to heat the drink a little more, in which case a microwave is perfect, or a small saucepan is required.
Stir the mixture to dissolve the honey, then drop in a slice of orange and dust with cinnamon.

Sip carefully, eat the orange slice, and allow the warmth to spread all the way to the tips of your fingers and toes.

❄

strawberry talisker

This cocktail of mine uses a medium smoky single malt from the Isle of Skye, Talisker.

INGREDIENTS

Strawberries, 6 small

Talisker 10-year-old Single Malt, 1½ shots (37.5 ml/1½ oz)

Crème de fraises de bois or strawberry liqueur, ½ shot (12.5 ml/½ oz)

Angostura bitters, dash

Sugar syrup, ⅓ shot (8 ml/⅓ oz)

METHOD

In a cocktail shaker, crush the strawberries. Add all the other ingredients and fill with ice. Shake as hard as you can to mix the strawberries through. Strain loosely into a martini glass.
No garnish.

Slurp generously, allowing the sweet fruit to slowly merge into the dry smoke of the whiskey.

whisky sour

This is one of the best known and loved refreshing whisky cocktails of all. You can make a whisky sour with whatever your favourite whisky is; the key is to slightly change the sugar content to match your whisky of choice. Scotch needs the most sugar, bourbon the least and rye somewhere in the middle.

INGREDIENTS

Dewar's 12-year-old Scotch, 2 shots (50 ml/2 oz)
Fresh lemon juice, I shot (25 ml/1 oz)
Sugar syrup, ⅓ shot (8 ml/⅓ oz)
Angostura bitters, dash
Egg white (optional), dash

METHOD

Add all the ingredients to a cocktail shaker. If you are including egg white, shake the shaker with NO ice first. This is a 'dry' shake and helps to aerate the liquid and create a thick foam.
After 'dry' shaking, or if you are not using egg white, fill the shaker with ice and shake hard. Now strain over ice in a large rocks glass.
Garnish with a maraschino cherry.

Drink at the club when you need to refresh and get away from the summer craziness.

smoked sour

This is one of my favourite variations on a whisky sour.

INGREDIENTS

Laphroaig 10-year-old Islay Single Malt or Lagavulin 16-year-old Islay Malt, 2 shots (50 ml/2 oz)

Fresh lemon juice, 1 shot (25 ml/1 oz)

Sugar syrup, ⅓ shot (8 ml/⅓ oz)

Angostura bitters, dash

Egg white (optional), dash

METHOD

Just like with a regular whisky sour, add all the ingredients to a cocktail shaker. If you are including egg white, shake the shaker with NO ice first. This is a 'dry' shake and helps to aerate the liquid and create a thick foam.
After 'dry' shaking, or if you are not using egg white, fill the shaker with ice and shake hard.
Now strain over ice in a large rocks glass. The lemon and smoky Islay malt are a fantastic flavour match, and the garnish I prefer is just a slice of lemon.

Drink on a summer evening after the heat of the day has started to subside, and you need something to wash the cares of the day away, too.

islay elixir

This is the cocktail that won me the 2008 Australian Bartender of the Year competition.

INGREDIENTS

Bowmore 10-year-old Islay Malt, 1½ shots (37.5 ml/1½ oz)

Yellow Chartreuse, ½ shot (12.5 ml/½ oz)

Carpano Antica Formula red vermouth, ½ shot (12.5 ml/½ oz)

Fee Brothers Barrel Aged Bitters (or Angostura), dash

METHOD

Add all ingredients to a mixing glass. Fill with ice and stir until the liquid and the ice have met in the middle. Strain into a chilled martini glass. Garnish with a twist of orange peel.

Drink before a hearty meal when the hint of bitterness will refresh your palate, and the sweetness will ease down the powerful single malt.

other cocktails

japanese slipper

This was first created in Melbourne, Australia, and is now available all over the world.

INGREDIENTS

Midori melon liqueur, 1 shot (25 ml/1 oz)
Cointreau, 1 shot (25 ml/1 oz)
Fresh lemon juice, 1 shot (25 ml/1 oz)

METHOD

Add all ingredients to a cocktail shaker. Fill with ice and shake like an Australian. Strain into a chilled martini glass. Garnish by dropping a maraschino cherry to the bottom of the glass.

Drink looking out over the Harbour Bridge in Sydney, or in a hidden lane-way bar in Melbourne.

voiron smash

This is one of my cocktails that I use to demonstrate that the power of green Chartreuse can be used for good as well as evil. Green Chartreuse is often abused by university students and other youngsters who value it for its excessive alcohol content. Unfortunately, this generally means that Chartreuse is relegated to a shot for those who want to get trashed, rather than the complex, sublime and delicious liqueur it really is in moderation.

INGREDIENTS

Green Chartreuse, 1½ shots (37.5 ml/1½ oz)
Pineapple, 4 chunks about 2.5 cm (1 in)
Mint, 6 leaves
Fresh lime juice, ½ shot (12.5 ml/½ oz)
Sugar syrup, ⅓ shot (8 ml/⅓ oz)

METHOD

In a cocktail shaker, muddle the pineapple and mint to get all the juice out. Add all the other ingredients and fill with ice. Shake really hard to mix through the pineapple and mint. Fine strain into a chilled martini glass to remove the pulp. Garnish with a mint leaf or slice of pineapple.

Sip and enjoy the six hundred years of tradition that goes into every bottle of green Chartreuse.

french martini

This is a cocktail that has gained huge popularity in the last few years. It can be a little sweet if made wrong, but when balanced right, it is delicious.

INGREDIENTS

42 Below Vodka, 1½ shots (37.5 ml/1½ oz)
Pineapple juice, 1 shot (25 ml/1 oz)
Chambord, ½ shot (12.5 ml/½ oz)

METHOD

Add all ingredients to a cocktail shaker. Fill with ice and shake extra hard and for a little longer than usual. Because there is no citrus component, you need a little extra water from the ice to balance the sweetness of the pineapple and Chambord. Strain into a chilled martini glass. No garnish.

Drink quickly with friends.

Bartender's Tip

Chambord is a French black raspberry liqueur and there is really no substitute, although Crème de Mûre works okay … If you make up some fresh pineapple juice, this drink becomes even better!

benedictine sour

This is a delicious variation on a whisky sour and shows that the sour recipe can be used with almost any base, even liqueurs.

INGREDIENTS

Benedictine, 2 shots (50 ml/1 oz)
Fresh lemon juice, 1 shot (25 ml/1 oz)
Egg white (optional), dash

METHOD

Add all ingredients to a cocktail shaker. If using egg white, 'dry' shake first, then fill with ice and shake again. If not using egg white, just fill with ice and shake hard. Strain over ice into a large rocks glass. Garnish with a maraschino cherry.

Drink before a formal dinner.

Bartender's Tip

Because of the sweetness in the Benedictine, you don't need to add any extra sugar.
Try this recipe with your favourite liqueur or spirit, adding a little sugar syrup if needed.

caipirinha

This is the national drink of Brazil. I was lucky to work with a lot of Brazilian students when I was making cocktails in London, and they all had their own local variation on this simple mixture. But at the heart of it are sugar, cachaça and fresh lime.

INGREDIENTS

Sagatiba Pura Cachaça, 2 shots (50 ml/2 oz)
Lime, 1 cut into eighths
White sugar, 2 tsp

METHOD

In a large rocks glass, muddle the sugar with the lime until it is completely crushed and ground.
Add the cachaça, two-thirds fill with crushed ice, and churn until the lime juice and sugar are completely mixed. Top with crushed ice. No garnish.

Drink with a salsa beat on a balmy evening.

Bartender's Tip

There are many different cachaças out there, and a good rule of thumb is to use brown sugar with a golden cachaça and white sugar with a white one. The recipe will give you a tart mix, so feel free to add a little more sugar, or sugar syrup, to match your preference.

bellini

This is one of the simplest and most delicious cocktails around. Created in Italy to go with the slightly sweeter prosecco sparkling wine, it will work perfectly well with champagne or any decent bubbles.

INGREDIENTS

Peach puree, ⅓ champagne flute
Prosecco, ⅔ champagne flute

METHOD

Pour in the peach puree and slowly, carefully, top with fizz. Give it a gentle stir. No garnish.

Drink at parties.

Bartender's Tip

This cocktail is even better in late spring when you can buy fresh white peaches and make your puree fresh. One trick to stop the peach puree turning brown: add a dash (½ shot/12.5 ml/½ oz) of fresh lemon juice.

the perfect party cocktail

The very best cocktails are those that have some connection to your life: drinks that have a historical significance that you identify with; drinks that you remember from a particular time, place or person. The very best cocktails are those that seem to capture a moment in time, and are able to take you back whenever you indulge. The Brazilians have a theory about this and how it relates to party cocktails. In Brazil, where cachaça and the caipirinha are the national drink, there is only one cocktail to be served at a party: the caipirinha jug. But the philosophy of this drink is very different from the normal intent with which we make cocktails. Where we attempt, and generally succeed, to recreate the exact flavour of a time or place, to reminisce and to return to happy memories, in Brazil the goal is to create something that can never be recreated.

The Brazilian party caipirinha starts its life like any other cocktail made in larger quantities. We begin with a large jug, add six to eight chopped limes depending on the size of the jug. Pour in some sugar, about 100g (3½ oz), and muddle until all the sugar has dissolved. Then pour in a bottle of cachaça. This should then be placed in the fridge to cool before the guests arrive. When people start arriving, add some ice to mixture and pour it out into glasses as required, allowing some lime pieces to fall into drinks as they will. When the jug is empty of liquid, there is usually some lime pieces left, do not wash or rinse it! Now the party caipirinha really begins. Add a few more limes, some more sugar, maybe a cut up mango or some peaches, whatever is on hand and in season. Muddle, until the sugar is melted, and pour in another bottle of cachaça. Add some ice, give it a quick stir and pour the mixture for your guests. When this runs dry, add more lime, some different fruit, more sugar, muddle and add cachaça and ice. Do not at any time wash or rinse the jug! The purpose is to allow the drink to evolve with the party, so that every batch is different and cannot be recreated. The philosophy behind this is that the drink represents a moment of that night, that party, that can never come again. To have tasted it, you had to be there.

five easy ways to impress your friendly neighbourhood bartender

Making friends with the bartender is a great way to get good drinks, great service and a friendly face when you pop in for a restorative. Below are some simple tips to help you make that connection.

- Don't drink what everyone else is drinking. This sets you apart and creates a chance for conversation.

- Ask the bartender what they like to drink, and if this sounds appealing, give it a go.

- Tequila and rum are always bartender favourites, but start by asking what their preferred brand is, because that will be different everywhere you go. With their favourite brand choice in mind, order a classic lime daiquiri, or a margarita with no salt, shaken.

- Another cheeky beverage that bartenders respect is a flavoured Polish vodka called Zubrowka. Pronounced roughly as zoo-brov-ka, it is flavoured with a special grass and tastes of hay with hints of clove, apple and vanilla. It goes really well with apple juice, and with soda and fresh lime. Even if the bar you are in does not stock it, most bartenders know it. Just don't lord it over the team if they have no idea — always be gracious.

- Tell the bartender what you have tasted and liked in the past, and ask them to create something similar for you.

about
the author

Sebastian Reaburn is one of Australia's best-known and most respected bartenders. After years of experience making cocktails in London, Sebastian returned to Melbourne, where he is now co-owner of 1806, one of Australia's most awarded cocktail bars. In the last five years he has won numerous accolades, the most recent being Best Cocktail List in the World at the 2008 Tales of the Cocktail festival in New Orleans and 2008 Australian Bartender of the Year.

Sebastian is a consistent finalist in national and global cocktail competitions. He continues studying, researching and presenting on cocktails, Molecular Mixology, customer service and new trends. Sebastian is often requested to present at bartender events and seminars, and holds seminars of his own on cutting-edge changes to the industry. He is a regular contributor to trade publications and mainstream media as a cocktail commentator.

Sebastian is still to be found behind the bar at 1806 when not training or travelling. He enjoys all spirits, with gin and tequila occasional favourites as the mood takes him. Sebastian is a fan of vinyl, mechanical watches, vintage cocktail shakers and, like most bartenders, Champagne.